CAMELS

IVING WILD

LIVING WILD

Published by Creative Education
P.O. Box 227, Mankato, Minnesota 56002
Creative Education is an imprint of The Creative Company
www.thecreativecompany.us

Design and production by Mary Herrmann
Art direction by Rita Marshall
Printed in the United States of America

Photographs by Alamy (Aurora Photos, blickwinkel, Franck Fotos, Hipix, imagebroker, MichaelGrantTravel, Moviestore collection Ltd, North Wind Picture Archives, Vic Pigula, Prisma Bildagentur AG, TGB, vario images GmbH & Co.KG), Dreamstime (Galyna Andrushko, Bertik, Blueximages, Christineg, Dmitry Dedyukhin, Dibrova, Fotomicar, Franfoto, Aleksandr Frolov, Hupeng, Attila Jandi, Joyfull, Katerika, Lian Deng, Mykhaylo Palinchak, Maxim Petrichuk, Rumos, Samrat35, Sigalpetersen, Tandemich, Wikkiss, Zoom-zoom), Getty Images (bravobravo, Jodi Cobb, Michael S. Lewis, Time & Life Pictures), iStockphoto (Clint Scholz), Shutterstock (Konstantin Kikvidze, Libor Piska)

Library of Congress Cataloging-in-Publication Data
Gish, Melissa.
Camels / by Melissa Gish.
p. cm. — (Living wild)
Includes bibliographical references and index.
Summary: A look at camels, including their habitats, physical characteristics such as their humps, behaviors, relationships with humans, and protected status of wild species in the world today.
ISBN 978-1-60818-166-7
1. Camels—Juvenile literature. I. Title.

QL737.U54G57 2012
599.63'62—dc23   2011035835

CPSIA: 061313 PO1705
9 8 7 6 5 4 3

CREATIVE EDUCATION

CAMELS

Melissa Gish

In Mongolia's vast Gobi Desert, a warm July wind swirls

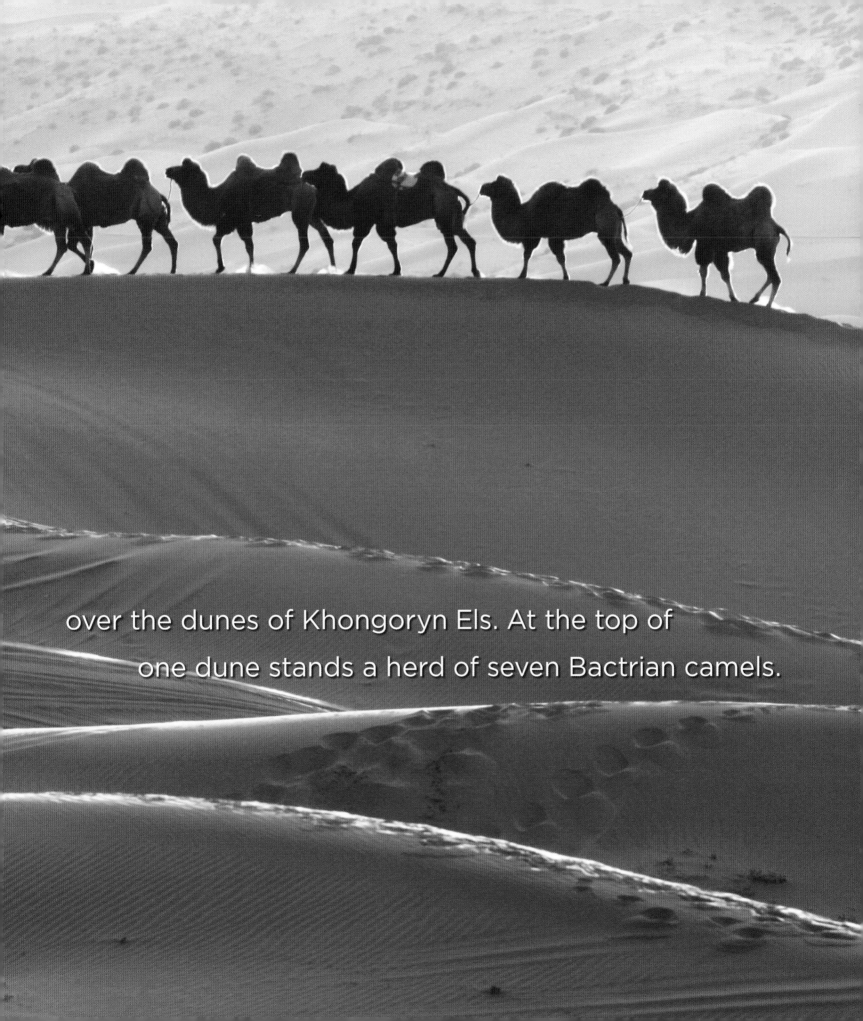

over the dunes of Khongoryn Els. At the top of
one dune stands a herd of seven Bactrian camels.

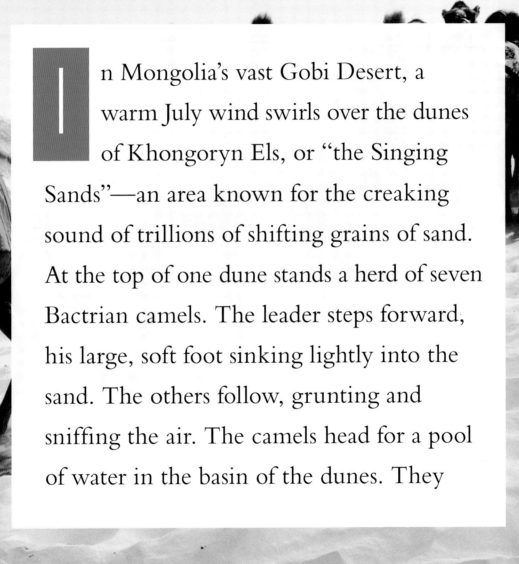

In Mongolia's vast Gobi Desert, a warm July wind swirls over the dunes of Khongoryn Els, or "the Singing Sands"—an area known for the creaking sound of trillions of shifting grains of sand. At the top of one dune stands a herd of seven Bactrian camels. The leader steps forward, his large, soft foot sinking lightly into the sand. The others follow, grunting and sniffing the air. The camels head for a pool of water in the basin of the dunes. They

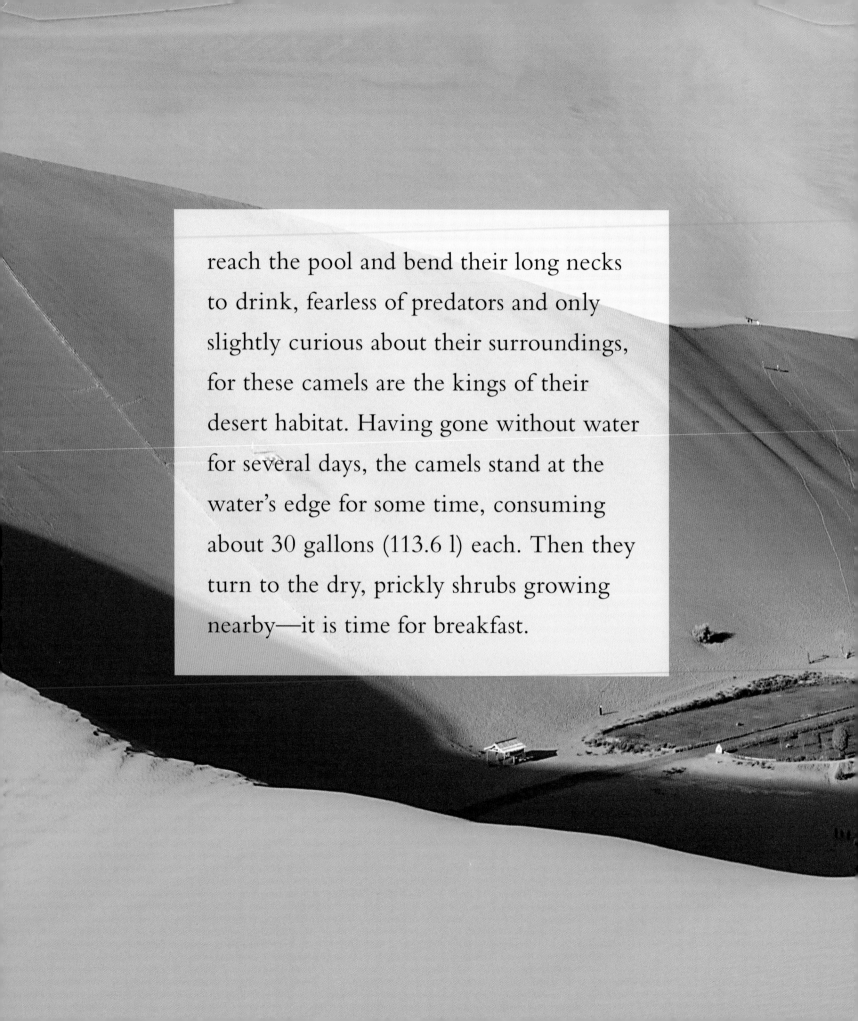

reach the pool and bend their long necks
to drink, fearless of predators and only
slightly curious about their surroundings,
for these camels are the kings of their
desert habitat. Having gone without water
for several days, the camels stand at the
water's edge for some time, consuming
about 30 gallons (113.6 l) each. Then they
turn to the dry, prickly shrubs growing
nearby—it is time for breakfast.

WHERE IN THE WORLD THEY LIVE

The two species of camel are suited to life in predominantly dry deserts or mountainous regions. Dromedaries inhabit parts of North Africa and the Middle East, while wild Bactrian camels are found in central Asia, northern China, and Mongolia. Feral dromedaries (originating from the Middle East) also live in central Australia today.

Dromedary
North Africa,
Middle East,
Australia

Bactrian Camel
central Asia,
northern China,
Mongolia

ONE HUMP OR TWO?

Wild camels are found only in North Africa, central Asia, and the Middle East. The earliest camel ancestors appeared about 40 million years ago and developed into dozens of species. However, only two species of camel exist today: dromedaries and Bactrian camels. Other members of the Camelidae family include the llamas, alpacas, guanacos, and vicuñas of South America. Camelids are physically characterized by their small heads and long legs and necks.

The camel's hump is its most striking feature. Dromedaries have one hump, and Bactrian camels have two humps. The humps are boneless and made of fleshy tissue. Camels store fat in their humps and can survive long periods of time without food or water when their humps are "full." When camels load up on food and water, thus creating stores of fat, the humps swell up and stiffen. As a camel's body draws on these reserves, its hump shrinks. In the case of Bactrian camels, the humps will flop over to one side when the fat stores have been depleted.

Both camel species stand six to seven feet (1.8–2.1 m) tall at the shoulder, and males are slightly larger than

Camels shed their winter coats in spring, producing four to seven pounds (1.8–3 kg) of valuable wool that is used to make clothing and rugs.

Nursing dromedaries lose weight, so they are not made to work until their young are weaned.

Camel milk has stopped the progression of human diabetes in test cases because it helps regulate the amount of sugar in blood.

females. The hump adds up to 12 more inches (30.5 cm) to a camel's height. Bactrian camels weigh 1,000 to 1,400 pounds (453–635 kg). Dromedaries' sizes vary according to their use, as most camels today are **domesticated**. Pack camels (those used to carry people and objects) can weigh up to 1,500 pounds (680 kg), while racing camels are typically less than half that size.

Our word "camel" comes from an Arabic word meaning "to bear." The dromedary's name is derived from the Greek word *dromas*, which means "running" and refers to the dromedary's ability to run swiftly. The Bactrian camel is named for Bactria—an ancient country that this camel once densely populated. Bactria no longer exists, but camels still inhabit the region of central Asia that includes Afghanistan, Tajikistan, and Uzbekistan. A small number of Bactrian camels are also found in northern China and Mongolia.

Camels and their relatives are mammals. All mammals, with the exceptions of the egg-laying platypus and the hedgehog-like echidnas, give birth to live offspring and produce milk to feed their young. Mammals are warm-blooded animals. This means that their bodies maintain a constant healthy temperature that is usually above that

A Bactrian camel's summer coat gets thicker until it is up to 10 inches (25 cm) long in winter.

Traditional camel saddles are made of leather-covered wood and are draped with woolen blankets.

of their surroundings. Camels live in extreme desert temperatures. Daytime summer temperatures can reach 140 °F (60 °C), and winter temperatures can plunge to -40 °F (-40 °C).

Camels adapt to these **fluctuations** by changing their own body temperature, heating up to 106 °F (41 °C) in the daytime and then cooling down to 93 °F (34 °C) at night. Most other animals could not survive such drastic daily changes in body temperature. Camels also gather together to remain cool or to get warmer.

A camel's dense, woolly fur helps keep it from getting sunburned. Dromedaries have white or light to tawny brown fur, and Bactrian camels are dark brown. Since dromedaries live where winters are mild, they have shorter fur than Bactrian camels, which grow shaggy winter coats to protect against snow and ice in their more northerly and mountainous habitats. A camel's eyes are shielded from the sun and dust by a double row of thick eyelashes. Bristly hairs in the ears keep sand from blowing in, as does the camel's ability to pinch its nostrils closed.

Camels are equipped with the long legs and broad feet that make travel across soft sand possible. Their wide feet

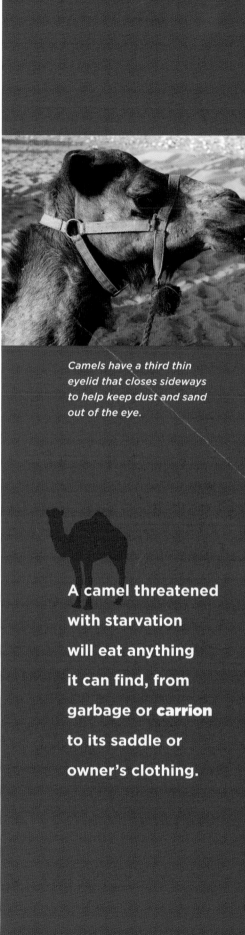

Camels have a third thin eyelid that closes sideways to help keep dust and sand out of the eye.

A camel threatened with starvation will eat anything it can find, from garbage or carrion to its saddle or owner's clothing.

Like horses, most camels' ages can be told by looking at their teeth, as an older camel's teeth will be more worn down.

have two toes, and the skin between the toes is loose. When camels walk through sand, their toes spread apart, stretching the skin and achieving an effect that is similar to a human walking on snowshoes through firmly packed snow. Leathery skin on the bottom of the feet protects the camel from hot sand. When it is resting with its legs tucked under its body, **calluses** over the leg joints and on the chest keep that skin protected, too.

Camels are herbivores, which means they eat only plants, leaves, grasses, seeds, and fruits. They get most of the moisture they need from their food. Many desert plants have thorns and prickly spines, and while most animals cannot eat such plants, camels have **adapted** to feed on them. Camels' tongues and the flesh inside their mouths are especially tough, preventing thorns and spines from puncturing them. In addition, a camel's upper lip is split into two halves that can move independently to carefully grasp food and maneuver it into the mouth. Camels have 34 teeth, but they have no front teeth in their upper jaw. They rip material from plants using the sharp front teeth in the lower jaw and the hard gums of the upper jaw. Then they grind the food using their back teeth, called molars.

Although camels' feet are made for walking on sand, the animals can get around fine on paved surfaces, too.

Domesticated camels may graze far from their camps, but, like cattle, they typically return in the evenings.

Camels have a special stomach—one with three chambers, or sections—that allows them to eat woody food such as twigs, which most other animals cannot digest. Food passes through the first chamber, called the rumen, where bacteria and acids soften it. Then the food is regurgitated, or brought back up to the mouth. This food mass, called a cud, is chewed again. When it is swallowed, the cud passes through all three stomach chambers to be fully digested. Camels share this trait of cud chewing with other animals called ruminants, such as cows, sheep, and giraffes. These other animals have four stomach chambers, but because camels have only three stomach chambers, they are not considered true ruminants.

A camel can eat about 9 pounds (4 kg) of food and drink about 50 gallons (189 l) of water per day. To reach a water source, camels may have to walk great distances. Camels walk slowly, but they can trot at speeds of about 12 miles (19 km) per hour for up to 18 hours without resting. Camels can run about 25 miles (40 km) per hour but can maintain that pace for only about 1 hour at a time. Racing dromedaries, on the other hand, can sprint up to 40 miles (64 km) per hour. Like racehorses, camels launch themselves through the air, lifting all four feet off the ground, when they run at full speed.

A camel cannot wear a bridle in its mouth as a horse does because its mouth must remain free to chew its cud.

Camels are called "ships of the desert" because a camel rider sways back and forth, resembling the motion of a ship at sea.

Unlike horses, domesticated dromedaries will kneel to help a rider get on or to allow cargo to be loaded.

Roughly 14 million dromedaries and 2 million Bactrian camels currently live as domestic animals. Fewer than 1,000 wild Bactrian camels are thought to still roam the deserts of northern China and Mongolia. Considered by scientists to be a subspecies separate from domestic Bactrian camels, these wild camels are among the rarest animals on Earth and are categorized as critically endangered by the International Union for Conservation of Nature (IUCN).

About one million **feral** dromedaries live in the deserts of central Australia. These camels are not native to Australia; they were brought from the Middle East to transport people and supplies while Australia was being explored and towns were being developed in the mid-1800s. Today's feral camels are descendants of camels that were abandoned by their original owners. Land resource managers in Australia consider these camels to be a **nuisance** because, having once been domesticated, the camels have no natural fear of humans. They will approach human settlements in search of water, even tearing up water supply lines in people's homes. Despite

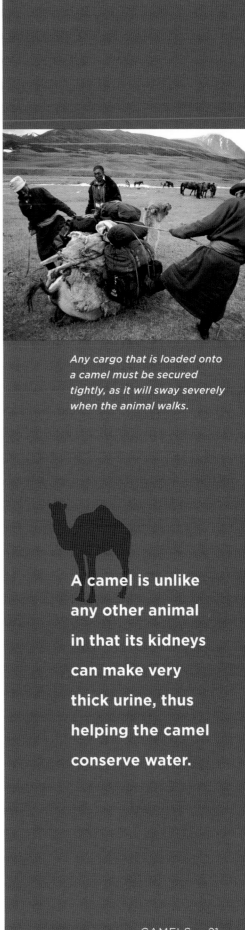

Any cargo that is loaded onto a camel must be secured tightly, as it will sway severely when the animal walks.

A camel is unlike any other animal in that its kidneys can make very thick urine, thus helping the camel conserve water.

being **nomadic**, the camels are overly abundant and can easily strip grazing land meant for sheep and cattle.

Domesticated camels are kept in pens, or enclosures, much like cattle. Males, called bulls, and females, called cows, are separated most of the time. In the wild, nomadic Bactrian bulls and cows remain apart for most of the year as they follow food and water sources. Where resources are plentiful, camels gather together in herds consisting of as many as 100 individuals. Most of the time, though, herds are made up of 2 to 15 members. Some herds consist of

only females and their young offspring. Bulls wander alone or gather in bachelor herds of all young males. There is no leadership in these herds, and members come and go, joining different herds throughout the year.

While camels can go days or weeks without food or water, they forage for food and consume water whenever these resources are available. When a camel has an adequate supply of moisture in its body, it will urinate often and drop **feces** that are moist. However, when water is scarce, a camel conserves water in its body by not

Despite their similar coloration, camels have unique facial expressions that can be recognized by their keepers.

Because camels are not territorial by nature, they will share food and water resources with each other.

urinating and by dropping feces that are hard and dry.

Camels locate water by smell. In desert habitats, water can be found at oases (*oh-AY-sees*). Vegetation grows in an oasis because water is present in the form of a spring or pond. Some oases are small and temporary, appearing and disappearing as the wind shifts sand dunes in the desert, but others, such as Crescent Lake Oasis in the Gobi Desert, are large and permanent. Camels instinctively do not remain at one oasis for long. They travel from place to place, which gives the vegetation at each oasis a chance to recover from being foraged by the camels.

Camels reach sexual maturity and are ready to mate around age five. Older camels, with their greater strength and experience, have advantages over younger camels when it comes to mating. During mating season, which is usually from late fall to early winter, a dominant bull begins gathering cows into his own herd. These herds, called harems, may contain up to 20 cows. To attract cows, a male groans and roars. Glands on the back of his head produce an oily substance that the camel rubs on his hump. He also urinates on his tail, which he then uses like a paintbrush to cover himself and his surroundings

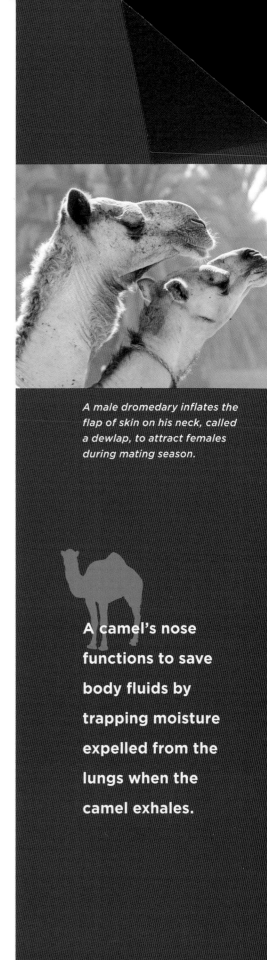

A male dromedary inflates the flap of skin on his neck, called a dewlap, to attract females during mating season.

A camel's nose functions to save body fluids by trapping moisture expelled from the lungs when the camel exhales.

Fighting males spit at and bite each other, and each may even try to sit on the other to show dominance.

Dromedaries and Bactrian camels can mate with one another, often producing offspring with the best qualities of each parent.

with his scent. Young bulls build their harems by invading existing harems and stealing young females. Bulls become highly aggressive during mating season and fight with each other to build or defend their harems. Camels push, twist their necks together, and bite each other while fighting. Injuries are common, but deaths are rare. One of the bulls typically gives up and walks away to end the fight.

A dominant bull will mate with members of only his harem. After about a month, the bull wanders away and leaves his cows to form their own herds again. Following a 13- to 14-month **gestation**, the pregnant cow will find a secluded place to give birth to a single calf. Twins are very rare. A newborn camel calf weighs an average of 70 pounds (32 kg) and stands about 3.5 feet (1 m) tall.

A calf is born with its eyes open. It is able to stand within a few hours of birth and immediately begins feeding on the milk produced by its mother. The calf is lighter colored than its mother, helping it blend in with its desert environment. After about three weeks, the mother will take her calf to join a herd of other camels. Although it begins eating vegetation at about three months of age, a calf depends on its mother's **nutrient**-rich milk for the first year of its life.

While adult camels have no predators other than humans, Bactrian camel calves are susceptible to attacks by snow leopards and wolves. Also, their nomadic lifestyle often takes a toll on young camels, who may not always be strong enough to keep up with the herd. Domestic calves sometimes suffer diseases and **parasitic** infections associated with confinement. Without human intervention and veterinary care, camels born in some regions have a high **mortality rate**. In rural areas of the Middle East, in particular, up to 20 percent of calves die before they reach 1 year old. A calf that survives its first year is called a yearling. Adult cows breed every other year, enabling yearlings to stay with their mothers for an additional 12 months, even if she is pregnant again.

At age two, the young camel is fully grown and capable of taking care of itself. A young bull will leave to join a bachelor herd, and a young cow will remain in her mother's herd. A wild Bactrian camel may live up to 30 years, and domesticated dromedaries and Bactrian camels can live another 20 years beyond that.

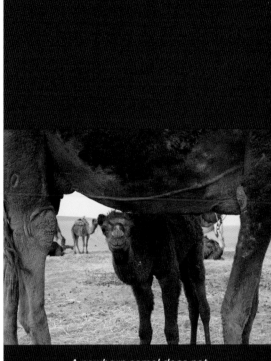

A newborn camel does not have a hump; the hump forms once the calf begins eating solid food.

As early as 206 B.C., camels were vital to travelers on the Silk Road, a collection of trade routes across Asia, Europe, and Africa.

CARAVANS AND CAMEL CORPS

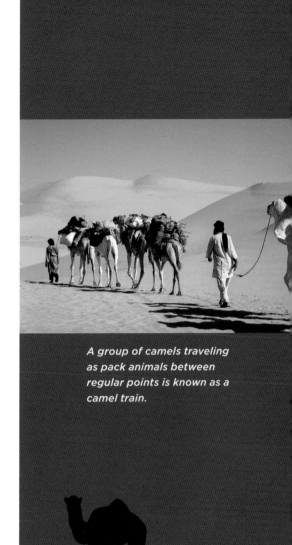

A group of camels traveling as pack animals between regular points is known as a camel train.

Camels have been part of desert peoples' cultures for thousands of years. As the only means of reliable transportation to Europe from Asia and the Middle East, camels were used to carry goods along trade routes. Like the leaders of wagon trains across the American West, traders and herdsmen led great caravans across the desert. These caravans comprised hundreds and sometimes thousands of camels laden with goods and travelers.

A healthy camel can carry up to 600 pounds (272 kg), and camels are still used today, though not as extensively, as pack animals. Like members of many nomadic cultures, the people of Kazakhstan think that traveling with camels offers protection from misfortune. The Kazakh people believe that killing a camel will bring death or disaster to the person committing this crime.

The Rabari of western India are known as the "camel people" because they have specialized in Bactrian camel breeding for hundreds of years. Their tradition tells that Shiva, the Hindu god of compassion and mercy, created the first Rabari person to be the keeper of the first camel,

Camels are safely able to lose up to 40 percent of the water in their blood—a condition that would be fatal in humans.

At more than 20 inches (51 cm) long, a camel's tail is ropelike with bristly hairs on the end and serves as a natural flyswatter.

which the goddess Parvati made from clay. While few camels now exist in India, the slaughtering and eating of a camel is still considered a serious offense in Rabari culture. The Rabari consume camel milk, but they never sell it, believing it is reserved for their people alone.

Camel racing is a popular sport throughout the Middle East, Mongolia, and even in Australia. Much like horses, camels are trained to run short distances at high speeds, carrying a **jockey**. Traditionally, jockeys in the Middle East were children, but this practice is changing, and even professional horse jockeys have been known to switch to riding camels. Some of the most famous camel races in the world include the annual King's Cup in Riyadh (*ree-YOD*), Saudi Arabia, and the annual Sheikh Zayed International Camel Endurance Race. Named for a former president of the United Arab Emirates who supported camel racing, the event sends captured and trained feral camels on a 93-mile (150 km) race across Australia's outback for a $50,000 prize.

For a short time, camels became part of the American landscape as well. The United States Army experimented with making camels a mode of transportation in the

Many countries are looking into replacing human riders with robotic jockeys because camel racing is so dangerous.

Hi Jolly died in what is now Quartzsite, Arizona, and a monument to him was constructed there in 1934.

Southwest during the mid-1800s, a time of conflicts with American Indians and Mexicans. In 1856, 20 years after Quartermaster Captain George H. Crosman first shared his ideas for using camels in the military, the U.S. Camel Corps was established. The army brought 33 camels from Turkey to the U.S. on a ship that landed at Indianola, Texas. Nine months later, 41 additional camels arrived.

Camel handlers led by a man named Hadji Ali (nicknamed "Hi Jolly") arrived from Turkey as well, and, together with 25 of the camels, they traveled under the direction of Lieutenant Edward Beale from Arizona to California in 1857. From 1859 to 1860, camels were part of a surveying team that mapped the Big Bend area of Texas. Despite the camels' problems with spooking horses and not responding well to American handlers, it seemed the Camel Corps had the potential for success.

Then, in 1861, America was torn apart with the onset of the Civil War, and the Camel Corps was used only to carry supplies to various army posts in the Southwest. In 1865, it was disbanded. Twenty-eight camels were given to the city of Los Angeles, California, to carry mail and baggage. The rest were sold—some bearing unborn calves—to miners and ranchers who wanted them as novelties. Many of these were subsequently sold to zoos, circuses, and traveling menageries—but others escaped into the desert, where they became feral.

The feral camels remained in the southern parts of Arizona, New Mexico, and Texas for many years. Topsy, the last documented offspring of the army camels, was captured while wandering in California and taken to the Griffith Park Zoo in Los Angeles, where she perished from old age in 1934. The last reported sighting of a feral camel was near the abandoned town of Douglas, Texas, in 1941. Many legends of the Southwest tell of ghostly camels still roaming the deserts.

One such creature, nicknamed the Red Ghost, is said to exist in Arizona. The tale emerged in 1883, when rumors circulated about a wild beast that trampled campsites, crushing people and leaving strands of reddish fur behind. Some people claimed the creature carried a headless rider upon its back. In 1893, a farmer shot and killed a feral camel believed to be the Red Ghost, but legend has it that this animal's spirit still haunts the Arizona desert.

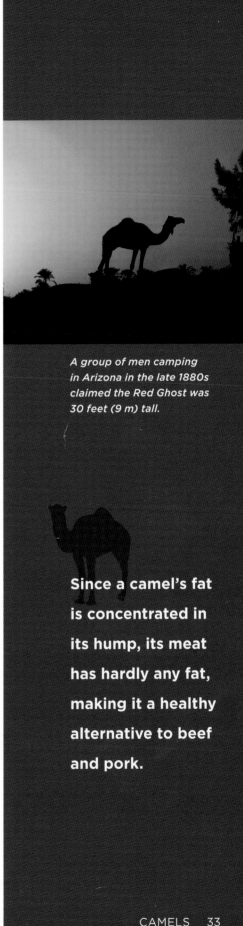

A group of men camping in Arizona in the late 1880s claimed the Red Ghost was 30 feet (9 m) tall.

Since a camel's fat is concentrated in its hump, its meat has hardly any fat, making it a healthy alternative to beef and pork.

Domesticated camels are prepared for service from a young age, carrying small loads on their backs.

A story from California relates how a gold prospector named Jake bought one of the army camels when they went up for auction. When word spread that Jake had struck gold, a man named Paul Adams crept into Jake's camp to murder and rob him. Jake's camel attacked Adams, who killed first the camel then Jake. Later, the ghosts of Jake and his camel chased Adams straight to the local sheriff, where the murderer confessed his crime. Some people believe that Jake and his phantom camel can still be seen in certain places.

Real-life camels are the subject of a German film called *The Story of Weeping Camel* (2003), about a nomadic family in Mongolia's Gobi region who raises a newborn Bactrian camel after its mother rejects it. Hollywood directors have borrowed trained camels for movies filmed in deserts, including *The Mummy* (1999), *The Mummy Returns* (2001), and *Sahara* (2005). Actors such as Matthew McConaughey have reported that riding a camel is nothing like riding a horse in the movies, as camels can be stubborn around strangers, making handling them a challenge.

Everyday people can experience camel rides in Moab, Utah. A vacation resort called the Camelot

Adventure Lodge takes visitors on camelback rides through Canyonlands National Park. Former Hollywood animal trainer Terry Moore cares for the resort's five dromedaries, and he taught one of the camels, Clyde, to lie down and play dead. Moore has said that camels are just like "big, loyal dogs."

Trained camels have appeared in hundreds of movies, including 2002's The Scorpion King.

Archaeological evidence suggests that the first Bactrian camels to be domesticated lived in what is now Iran around 2600 B.C.

TOO MANY, TOO FEW

About 46 million years ago, the first camelid ancestors **evolved** in North America. *Poebrodon* was part of a growing group of hoofed, grass-eating animals that spread across the continent. Scientists estimate these creatures weighed between 3,500 and 5,500 pounds (1,588–2,495 kg). About 30 to 20 million years ago, the much smaller *Gentilicamelus* evolved. This camelid stood about 3.2 feet (.9 m) high and weighed less than 200 pounds (91 kg). Over the millennia, camelids began to grow larger again. The 10-foot-tall (3 m) *Aepycamelus* existed from about 10 million to 5 million years ago.

During one of Earth's ice ages, about three million years ago, some of these early camelids migrated to South America, where they became the modern camel's relatives. The camelids that remained in North America eventually died out but not before some of them crossed the Bering **Land Bridge** from North America into Siberia. These animals flourished and spread south across Asia, where they evolved into the short-haired dromedary of the Middle Eastern deserts and the long-haired

North African and Middle Eastern languages have hundreds of words describing camels, including the Somali *gool*, for "fat camel."

Motorists in Australia are warned to be on the lookout for such animals as camels, kangaroos, and wombats.

Bactrian camel of the Asian steppes, the treeless grasslands of Mongolia and Kazakhstan.

Around two million years ago, the two camel species we know today roamed their current habitats; thousands of years later, they coexisted peacefully with humans. While cattle were domesticated about 10,000 years ago, camels were domesticated only about 4,000 years ago. Better suited than cattle to carrying heavy loads over long distances, camels played an important role in human urban development, or the building of cities and towns, as well as in exploration and the expansion of trade routes. Because populations of domesticated camels are high today, conservation efforts for these camels are virtually nonexistent. In fact, just the opposite is true in Australia, where feral camels have become overly abundant and are in need of management.

A major concern of conservationists is that camels may be grazing native plant species to extinction. From 2005 to 2008, a wildlife research group in Australia called Ninti One undertook a comprehensive study of feral camels to determine both the camels' specific effects on the natural environment and the best strategies to manage them. Many of Ninti One's recommendations have been put

into practice, including one method of population control that provides immediate results: culling, or killing off a portion of the feral camel population. The camels are sold for their meat, with a portion of the proceeds going to support the restoration of **Aboriginal** communities affected by the camels' destruction of the native ecosystem.

Wild Bactrian camels are studied as much as Australia's feral camels but for a very different reason. Among the most endangered mammals on the planet, the Bactrian camel is in desperate need of conservation to save it from extinction. Interestingly, the camels survived deadly radiation from decades of **nuclear** testing in the Gobi Desert, but now they have been pushed to the edge of extinction by humans invading their desert habitat.

The last remaining wild Bactrian camels on Earth are dependent on the efforts of conservationists and scientists.

Australian feral camels tend to be darker in color and have denser fur than their Middle Eastern counterparts.

Most Mongolians, especially those who depend upon it for livelihood or resources, greatly respect the Bactrian camel.

The Zoological Society of London sponsors a program called EDGE of Existence, which is dedicated to the study of the "evolutionarily distinct and globally endangered," or one-of-a-kind species approaching extinction. Bactrian camels are number 13 on EDGE's list of most endangered mammals. Through its involvement in educational programs and research projects such as those conducted by the Captive Wild Camel Breeding Centre in Zakhyn Us, Bayan Toroi, Mongolia, EDGE seeks to encourage progress in camel research.

The greatest threats to Bactrian camels are human interference and hunting. Although land was set aside by the Mongolian government in 1982 for the purpose of preserving the Bactrian camel and other threatened and endangered species, posted signs around the region keep few trespassers away. The United Nations Educational, Scientific and Cultural Organization (UNESCO) established the Great Gobi Biosphere as a protected area, yet every year, hundreds of people enter the region to illegally mine gold and iron ore, disrupting wild Bactrian camel habitat. The Mongolian government does not have the resources or the manpower to monitor the reserves, which are about the size of Texas; therefore, many illegal activities go unreported, while camels and other wildlife suffer the consequences of litter, water contamination, destruction of plants and grasses, and **poaching**.

Experts estimate that at least 20 camels in the Gobi are killed annually for their meat. In addition, when humans disturb natural water sources by polluting or emptying oases, predation of camels increases. Gobi wolves rarely attack camels, but when these two species find themselves at the same few remaining watering holes at the same time, conflict is inevitable. Mining produces substances, such as potassium cyanide, that poison camels, and vehicles can destroy important food sources. Also, many people who illegally move into protected areas bring with them goats that compete with camels for grazing land and water.

One of the camels' most uncompromising advocates is Dr. Pamela Burger from the Institute of Animal Breeding and **Genetics** at the University of Veterinary Medicine in Vienna, Austria. She studied wild Bactrian camels in the Gobi Desert for a number of years and now supervises the research of other scientists in Mongolia. Burger's team works in collaboration with

In China, Mongolia, and parts of eastern Russia, Bactrian camels have also been called snow camels.

Even wild Bactrian camels are cautious but not fearful of humans and seldom flee when approached.

Each day, a female camel can produce 5 to 10 gallons (19–38 l) of milk that is more nutrient-rich than cow or goat milk.

Dr. Han Jianlin of the Beijing Genomics Research Institute in China to record and study the genetic data of all remaining wild Bactrian camels to determine how many of them are genetically pure and how many are mixes of domestic Bactrian camels and dromedaries.

Genetic research is essential in designing **captive-breeding** programs geared toward preserving wild Bactrian camels. In 2004, the Wild Camel Protection Foundation established the Hunter Hall Captive Wild Camel Breeding Centre in Zakhyn Us, Mongolia. The center's population of 12 camels has now more than doubled. Within the coming decade, the center plans to initiate the first release of wild camels back into the Gobi Desert, where these noble nomads of the desert can be free to rebuild their population.

While domestic camels are valuable to people from many cultures for many purposes, from transportation to entertainment, wild camels are equally important members of their Asian ecosystems. Continued research on and education about the needs and habits of wild camels will be essential to preserving these fascinating animals. While camels can thrive in conditions few other animals can tolerate, their ultimate survival depends on us.

Camel hair is collected and spun into wool to make clothing items, such as waterproof coats, and carpet backing.

ANIMAL TALE: BUDDHA BUILDS THE CAMEL

Despite its strange appearance, the camel is treasured by the people of central Asia for its gentle nature and cultural significance. This tale from Mongolia explains how the Bactrian camel became tied to the Chinese religious figure Buddha and the Chinese zodiac, or the 12 animal symbols of the Chinese calendar.

Long ago, when the Buddha made the calendar, he assigned an animal to each of the 12 parts of the Buddhist calendar. After he had selected 11 animals, the Buddha looked around, trying to decide who should become the 12th animal. The camel and the rat, eager to be selected, approached the Buddha to beg for the final spot on the calendar.

"You are both worthy candidates," said the Buddha after listening to the pleas of the rat and the camel. "This will not be an easy choice. I propose you hold a contest."

The rat and the camel discussed all manner of possibilities. Finally, the rat proposed, "Whichever of us sees the first ray of light in the morning will represent the final year of the calendar."

"That sounds like a fine idea," replied the camel. And with that, he turned to the east and settled down in the middle of a broad, open desert. From this position, he believed, he would surely be the first to see the morning sun.

The rat asked the camel if he could sit on the camel's back. The camel thought this was strange, but he agreed. The rat scrambled up to the top of the camel's back—and turned to the west toward the high, snow-capped mountains.

"You silly rat," the camel said, turning to look at his rival. "Don't you know that the sun rises in the east?"

"That it does," replied the rat, fluffing up the camel's fur to make a comfortable pillow. "That it does."

The camel simply shook his head and returned to his watch, staring intently into the east for the first signs of morning. Hours passed, and then the sun began to rise. The camel looked to the eastern horizon, waiting. Suddenly, a slender sliver of light struck a tall, snowy mountaintop to the west.

"I saw it," cried the rat. "I saw it right there!" He was jumping up and down, pointing to the west. The camel turned his head—and there he saw the first rays of sunlight bouncing off the tall mountaintops. He turned his head back to the east, and in that instant the orange orb rose over the eastern horizon.

"Unbelievable!" shouted the camel, shaking the rat off his back. "How is this possible?"

"The sun always strikes the mountains before it strikes the desert," said the rat. "You should have known that."

The Buddha, witnessing this exchange, rewarded the clever rat with the top spot on the calendar. But to the camel he gave the characteristics of all the animals of the calendar:

the small ears of the rat
the chambered stomach of the cow
the broad feet of the tiger
the soft nose of the rabbit
the humped back of the dragon
the wool of the sheep
the teeth of the horse
the forehead of the ape
the beard of the rooster
the crooked legs of the dog
and the wiry-haired tail of the pig

GLOSSARY

Aboriginal – of or relating to the Australian Aborigines, the people who inhabited Australia before the arrival of European settlers

adapted – changed to improve its chances of survival in its environment

calluses – layers of thickened and enlarged tough or leathery skin

captive-breeding – being bred and raised in a place from which escape is not possible

carrion – the rotting flesh of an animal

domesticated – tamed to be kept as a pet or used as a work animal

evolved – gradually developed into a new form

feces – waste matter eliminated from the body

feral – in a wild state after having been domesticated

fluctuations – irregular risings and fallings in number or amount

genetics – relating to genes, the basic physical units of heredity

gestation – the period of time it takes a baby to develop inside its mother's womb

jockey – a person whose job is to ride on the back of an animal in a competitive race

land bridge – a piece of land connecting two landmasses that allowed people and animals to pass from one place to another

mortality rate – the number of deaths in a certain area or period

nomadic – relating to a group of people or animals with no fixed home who move, often according to the seasons, in search of food, water, or grazing land

nuclear – relating to the energy released from the splitting of atoms, or very small particles of matter

nuisance – something annoying or harmful to people or the land

nutrient – a substance that gives an animal energy and helps it grow

parasitic – being an animal or plant that lives on or inside another living thing (called a host) while giving nothing back to the host; some parasitic organisms cause disease or even death

poaching – hunting protected species of wild animals, even though doing so is against the law

SELECTED BIBLIOGRAPHY

Aulagnier, S., Patrick Haffner, A. J. Mitchell-Jones, Francois Moutou, and J. Zima. *Mammals of Europe, North Africa, and the Middle East*. London: A & C Black, 2009.

Hare, John. *Mysteries of the Gobi: Searching for Wild Camels and Lost Cities in the Heart of Asia*. London: I. B. Taurus, 2009.

National Geographic. "Arabian (Dromedary) Camel." http:// animals.nationalgeographic.com/animals/mammals/ dromedary-camel.html.

Reading, Richard P., Dulamtserengiin Enkhbileg, and Tuvdendorjiin Galbaatar, eds. *Ecology and Conservation of Wild Bactrian Camels*. Denver: Denver Zoological Foundation Series in Conservation Biology, 2002.

San Diego Zoo. "Animal Bytes: Camel." http://www .sandiegozoo.org/animalbytes/t-camel.html.

Wild Camel Protection Foundation. "Wild Bactrian Camels." http://www.wildcamels.com/bactrian-camels.

Like people who own and care for horses, camel keepers form close relationships with their animals.

INDEX